A

of Blessed
Mother Teresa
of Calcutta

Compiled and introduced by
Don Mullan

First published in 2003 by

the columba press

55A Spruce Avenue, Stillorgan Industrial Park,
Blackrock, Co Dublin
Reprinted 2004

Designed by Bill Bolger
Cover photo by kind permission of
Edizioni San Paolo/S. Ballini
Origination by The Columba Press
Printed in Ireland by
ColourBooks Ltd, Dublin

ISBN 1 85607 428 5

To
Moya, Liam, Cathal and Deirdre
and to their families and friends

Acknowledgements:

The publisher and editor gratefully acknowledge the permission of Sr M. Nirmala, Superior General, Missionaries of Charity, Mother House, Calcutta, to quote from material in their copyright: Nobel Prize Acceptance Speech 1979, Oslo, Norway; Address to the National Prayer Breakfast, Washington, DC, 3 February 1994; Quotations of Mother Teresa sent to Don Mullan in Letter from Sr M. Nirmala, MC, 17 August 2003; Don Mullan, interview with Mother Teresa, Dublin, 8 July 1981; *Wisdom from Mother Teresa of Calcutta*, St Mary-the-Virgin PCC, March 2001 Magazine; *A Guide to Daily Living with Mother Teresa: The Joy in Loving*, compiled by Jaya Chaliha and Edward Le Jolym (Penguin Group, New York 1996); *Something Beautiful for God* by Malcolm Muggeridge, William Collins Sons & Co Ltd (1971).

Author's Acknowledgements

Sincere thanks are owed to the following for their kind support and assistance with this publication:

Sr Luca, Missionaries of Charity, Dublin, Ireland; Sr Lawrence, Missionaries of Charity, London, England; Sr Paula Marie, Missionary of Charity, Calcutta, India; Sr M. Nirmala, Superior General, Missionaries of Charity, Mother House, Calcutta, India, for her very kind permission to publish this collection of quotations from Mother Teresa with the following words: 'For the glory of God and the good of the people, we are happy to give you permission to use all the quotations ...'; Gary

Burke, RIP, who departed this life on 7 March 2003; to Frank Burke and A Gift of Roses Trust for their openness and support; Bernie Bergin for her assistance with parallel reading and continued great goodwill, humour and friendship; to the late Mary Walshe, a tireless friend and co-worker of Mother Teresa who kindly arranged my interview with Mother Teresa in Dublin on 8 July 1981; to Dr John Magee, Bishop of Cloyne, who kindly arranged meetings with Mother Teresa in Rome in 1981; to Seán O Boyle and the staff of Columba Press; Seamus Cashman who planted the seed of this Little Book series; and last but not least, my family: Margaret, Thérèse, Carl and Emma for their continued patience, understanding, kindness and warmth.

INTRODUCTION

On 8 July 1981 I had the privilege of
meeting and interviewing Mother Teresa
of Calcutta in Dublin. Several of the
quotations throughout this book are taken
directly from that interview. I met her on
three other occasions in Dublin and
Rome. One of those was a private, per-
sonal encounter, during which I sought
her advice about an important life decision
I had to make. She was totally present
and available and I have never regretted
the decision I made following our
encounter. While Mother Teresa continu-
ally expressed the hope that both she and

everyone would do 'Something Beautiful for God' in truth she *was* 'Something Beautiful from God'. Even unbelievers were moved by the light of love and human compassion that radiated from her being.

She was born on 26 August 1910 in Skopje, Albania (now the capital of Macedonia) to a devout mother and a father who was a well-respected local businessman. She was baptised Agnes Gonxha Bojaxhiu the following day. At the age of 12 she knew that she wished to serve the poor, eventually making India her choice. Aged 18 she left home and

travelled to Dublin to begin her novitiate
with the Irish Sisters of Loreto, before
travelling to Calcutta where she took her
primary vows. She chose the religious
name 'Teresa' after St Thérèse of Lisieux.

From 1929 to 1946 Mother Teresa
served as a teacher in Calcutta during
which she experienced 'a call within a
call'. It was a call to dedicate the remain-
der of her religious life to serving the
poorest of the poor. By 1950 she was
given permission to found the *Missionaries
of Charity*, a religious order whose
primary purpose is to serve God in the
distressing disguise of the poor. The

Order's heroic work in the slums of India and throughout the world earned Mother Teresa the name 'Saint of the gutters' and for which she received the 1979 Nobel Peace Prize. She died in her beloved Calcutta on Friday, 5th September 1997, aged 87.

Pope John Paul II beatified Mother Teresa in Rome on *Mission Sunday*, 19th October 2003.

Don Mullan
Dublin
1 October 2003
Feast of St Thérèse of Lisieux

Quotations from
Blessed Mother Teresa
of Calcutta

LET US BEGIN

Yesterday is gone.
Tomorrow has not yet come.
We have only today.
Let us begin.

THE ONLY CONDITION

This is the only condition
that Christ really places on us:
'Love one another as I have loved you.'
And we know very well how much
he loved us!
He died for us!

THE HOLY SPIRIT

The Spirit pours love, peace, joy
into our hearts proportionately to our
emptying ourselves of self-indulgence,
vanity, anger and ambition,
and to our willingness to
shoulder the Cross of Christ.

MARY OUR MOTHER

Mary our Mother,
give us your heart,
so beautiful, so pure, so immaculate.
Your heart so full of love and humility …

MARY OUR MOTHER

Give us your heart
that we may be able to receive Jesus
in the Bread of Life,
Love him as you loved him
and serve him
in the distressing disguise of the poor.

MARY OUR MOTHER

How much we can learn from our Lady!
She was so humble
because she was all for God.
She was full of grace.

GOD'S GRACE

Make sure that you let God's grace
work in your souls
by accepting whatever he gives you,
and giving him
whatever he takes from you.

Something Beautiful for God

What you are doing
I cannot do.
What I am doing
You cannot do.
But together we are doing
something beautiful for God.

LOVE THY NEIGHBOUR

Because we cannot see Christ
we cannot express our love to him;
but our neighbours we can always see,
and we can do to them what
if we saw him
we would like to do to Christ.

THE DIGNITY OF THE POOR

They are very great people.
They are very loveable people.
They have tremendous love
for their family life,
for their children.
They are always sharing.

THE POOR

It doesn't matter how little they have,
they're always ready to share
with somebody who has nothing
or who is poorer than they.
That is the greatness of the poor.

THE POOR

Christ is hidden
under the suffering appearance
of anyone who is hungry,
anyone who is naked,
anyone who is homeless or dying.

THE POOR

Let us not be satisfied
with just giving money.
Money is not enough,
money can be got,
but they need your hearts to love them.
So, spread your love everywhere you go.

THE POOR

If I had not picked up
that first person dying on the street,
I would not have picked up
the thousands later on.

THE COURAGE TO SHARE
A Story

A gentleman came to our house
and told me:
'There is a Hindu family
with eight children.
They have not eaten for some time.'
So I took some rice
and I went to the family.

The Courage to Share

The mother took the rice from me
And she divided it into two
and she went out …
She knew the Muslim family next door
were hungry too
and she had the courage to share.

The Courage to Share

I was not surprised that she gave.
But I was surprised that she knew.
There was this greatness.
She had time to think of others.

THE EUCHARIST

It is so beautiful to connect
the Eucharist with the poor.
Jesus is the Bread of Life
and Jesus in the broken bodies of the poor
is the same Jesus.
He said,
'As you did it to me, it was I the hungry
one.'

The Eucharist

In Holy Communion we have Christ
under the appearance of bread.
In our work we find him
under the appearance of flesh and blood.
It is the same Christ.
'I was hungry, I was naked, I was sick,
I was homeless.'

THE SIN OF INDIFFERENCE

The sin of indifference is omission,
where we don't bother
and don't care.

The Sin of Indifference

Indifference is because
we don't know the love of Jesus
or we have lost contact with him.

The Sin of Indifference

So we don't know,
or we don't want to know,
or we don't care to know.

SIN

Sin is an offence against the love of God
and we hurt Jesus
each time we commit sin.

THOUGHTFULNESS

Thoughtfulness
is the beginning of great sanctity.

THOUGHTFULNESS

If you learn the art of being thoughtful,
you will become
more and more Christ-like,
for his heart was meek
and he always thought of others.

JESUS

Jesus made himself bread of life
to satisfy our hunger for God's love
because we have been created to love
and to be loved.

JESUS

Jesus made himself the hungry one
so that we would be able
to satisfy his hunger
with our human love.

JESUS

Jesus has made himself the hungry one,

The naked one,

The homeless one,

So that we can,

by our work

amongst the poorest of the poor,

satisfy his hunger for our love.

JESUS

I believe in person to person.
Every person is Christ for me,
and since there is only one Jesus,
that person is the one person in the world
at that moment.

JESUS

There are so many religions
and each one has its different ways
of following God.
I follow Christ:
Jesus is my God,
Jesus is my Spouse,
Jesus is my life,
Jesus is my only love,
Jesus is my all in all;
Jesus is my everything.

JESUS

The dying,
the cripple,
the mentally handicapped,
the unwanted,
the unloved
– they are Jesus in disguise.

JESUS

Put yourself completely under
the influence of Jesus,
so that he may think his thoughts
in your mind,
do his work through your hands,
for you will be all-powerful
with him who strengthens you.

JESUS

Jesus wanted to help by sharing our life,
our loneliness, our agony, our death.
Only by being one with us
has he redeemed us.

FAITHFULNESS

Be faithful in small things
because it is in them
that your strength lies

FAITHFULNESS

I do not pray for success.
I ask for faithfulness.

FAITH

Faith is a gift of God.
Without it there would be no life.
Love and faith go together,
they complete each other.

HOPE

Hope is a gift of God.
If you love then you have hope.
You see, if someone doesn't love,
then she has no hope.

HOPE

Faith, hope and love
are all connected together
and you can't have one without the other.

LOVE

The chance to share our love
with others is
a gift from God.

LOVE

Intense love does not measure;
it just gives.

LOVE

Spread love everywhere you go:
First of all in your house.

LOVE

The most terrible poverty
is loneliness
and the feeling of being unloved.

LOVE

There is more hunger
for love and appreciation
in this world
than for bread.

LOVE UNTIL IT HURTS

I have found the paradox
that if I love until it hurts,
then there is no hurt,
but only more love.

LOVE UNTIL IT HURTS

We cannot all do great things,
but we can do small things
with great love.

LOVE UNTIL IT HURTS

If we really want to love,
we must learn to forgive
before anything else.

LOVE UNTIL IT HURTS

Let us more and more insist
on raising funds of love,
of kindness,
of understanding,
of peace.
The rest will be given.

LOVE UNTIL IT HURTS

Love for my neighbour
will lead me to true love for God.

LOVE UNTIL IT HURTS

Let's Love one another;
that will accomplish miracles.

THE UNBORN

If we accept that a mother
can kill her own child,
how can we tell other people
not to kill one another?

The Unborn

That unborn child has been carved
in the hand of God from conception
and is called by God
to love and to be loved,
not only now in this life, but forever.

THE UNBORN

It is a poverty
to decide that a child must die
so that you may live as you wish.

THE UNBORN

How do we persuade a woman
not to have an abortion?
As always, we must persuade her with love,
and we remind ourselves that love means
to be willing to give until it hurts.

The Family

Make time for each other in your family.

THE FAMILY

It is easy to love people far away.
It is not always easy
to love those close to us.

The Family

It is easier to give a cup of rice
to relieve hunger
than to relieve the loneliness and pain
of someone unloved in our own home.

The Family

Bring love into your home
for this is where
our love for each other must start.

The Family

Love begins at home.

Unwanted

I have come more and more to realise
that being unwanted
is the worst disease
that any human being can ever experience.

KINDNESS

Be the living expression
of God's kindness …
kindness in your face
kindness in your eyes
kindness in your smile
kindness in your warm greeting.

KINDNESS

Mary can teach us kindness –
she went in haste
to serve Elizabeth.

KINDNESS

I prefer you to make mistakes in kindness
than work miracles in unkindness.

KINDNESS

Be kind and merciful.
Let no one ever come to you
without coming away better and happier.

LISTEN

Listen in silence
because if your heart
is full of other things,
you cannot hear the voice of God.

LISTEN

The more we receive in silent prayer,
the more we can give in our active life.

LISTEN

We need silence to be able to touch souls.

LISTEN

The essential thing is not what we say,
but what God says to us
and through us.

LISTEN

All our words will be useless
unless they come from within.

LISTEN

Words
which do not give the light of Christ
increase the darkness.

A Smile

Let us always meet each other with a
smile,
for the smile is a beginning of love.

A Smile

Smile at each other,
smile at your wife,
smile at your husband,
smile at your children,
smile at each other –
it doesn't matter who it is –
and that will help you to grow up
in greater love for each other.

A Smile

We shall never know
all the good that
a simple smile can do.

A Smile

True holiness consists
in doing God's
will with a smile.

JOY

God is joy.
God is love.
A Sister filled with joy
preaches without preaching.

JOY

Joy is prayer
Joy is strength
Joy is love.
Joy is a net of love
by which you can catch souls.
God loves a cheerful giver.

PEACE

Let us not use bombs and guns
to overcome the world.
Let us use love and compassion.

Let us preach the peace of Christ
as he did.
He went about doing good.

PEACE

If everyone could see the image of God
in his neighbour,
do you think we should still need
tanks and generals?

PEACE

If we have no peace
it is because we have forgotten
that we belong to each other.

PEACE

If you want to make peace
you don't talk to your friends.
You talk to your enemies.

PRAYER

Love to pray –
feel often during the day
the need for prayer,
and take trouble to pray.

PRAYER

Prayer enlarges the heart
until it is capable of containing
the gift of God.

PRAYER

Ask and seek,
and you heart will grow big enough
to receive God
and keep him as your own.

ONE GOD

There is only one God
and he is God to all.
Therefore it is important
that everyone is seen as equal before God.

ONE GOD

I've always said
we should help a Hindu
become a better Hindu,
a Muslim become
a better Muslim,
a Catholic become
a better Catholic.
We believe our work
should be our example to people.

One God

God has his own ways and means
to work in the hearts of human beings.
We do not know
how close people are to God…
if the individual thinks and believes that
this is the only way to God for her or him,
this is the way God comes into their life.

ONE GOD

We have among us 475 souls –
30 Catholics and the rest
Hindus, Muslims, Sikhs –
all different religions.
But they all come to our prayers.

ONE GOD

Religion is the worship of God,
therefore a matter of conscience.
I alone must decide for myself
and you for yourself what we choose.

HEAVEN ON EARTH

We all long for heaven where God is,
but we have it in our power
to be in heaven with God right now –
to be happy with him
at this very moment.

HEAVEN ON EARTH

But being happy with God now means:

Loving as he loves,

Helping as he helps,

Giving as he gives,

Serving as he serves,

Rescuing as he rescues,

Being with him twenty-four hours,

Touching him

in his distressing disguise of the poor.

Heaven on Earth

Only in heaven we will see
how much we owe to the poor
for helping us to love God better
because of them.

Forgiveness and Humility

Before we forgive
we must know
that we need forgiveness.

FORGIVENESS AND HUMILITY

We need lots of love to forgive
But we need lots of humility to forget.

FORGIVENESS AND HUMILITY

If we can obtain the graces
of forgiveness and humility
there will be
peace, happiness, joy and unity
in our homes and on earth.

SAINTLINESS

'I will be a saint' means
I will despoil myself
of all that is not God.

SAINTLINESS

'I will be a saint' means
I will strip my heart of all created things;
I will live in poverty and detachment.

SAINTLINESS

'I will be a saint' means
I will renounce my will,
my inclinations,
my whims and fancies,
and make myself a willing slave
to the will of God.

Do not wait

Do not wait for leaders.
Do it alone,
person-to-person.

JUST ONE

If you can't feed a hundred people
then feed just one.

GOD'S PENCIL

We are all pencils
in the hand of God.

JUST A DROP

We sometimes feel
that what we do
is just a drop in the ocean.
But the ocean would be less
because of that missing drop.

Our Work

Our work is God's work and to remain so,
all of us are but instruments,
who do our little bit and pass by.

GOD'S WORK

Christ's life was not written
during his lifetime,
yet he did the greatest work on earth –
he redeemed the world and taught
humankind to love his Father.

GOD'S WORK

Our work is only the expression
of the love we have for God.
We have to pour our love on someone.
And the people are the means
of expressing our love for God.

Breaking of the Heart

A Story
I once picked up a woman
from a garbage dump
and she was burning with fever;
she was in her last days
and her only lament was:
'My son did this to me'.

Breaking of the Heart

I begged her: 'You must forgive your son.

In a moment of madness,

when he was not himself,

he did a thing he regrets.

Be a mother to him, forgive him.'

Breaking of the Heart

It took me a long time to help her say:
'I forgive my son.'
Just before she died in my arms,
she was able to say that
with a real forgiveness.

BREAKING OF THE HEART

She was not concerned
that she was dying.
The breaking of the heart
was that her son did not want her.
This is something you and I
can understand.

In God's Mind

God can never forget us.

The Good Fruit

The Good Fruit

The fruit of silence
is prayer;

The Good Fruit

The fruit of prayer
is faith;

THE GOOD FRUIT

The fruit of faith
is love;

The Good Fruit

The fruit of love
is service;

THE GOOD FRUIT

The fruit of service
is peace.

PEACE

Find Jesus and you will find peace.

Last Words of Mother Teresa

Jesus, I love you;

Jesus, I trust you;

Jesus, I love you;

Jesus, I trust you ...